21-Day Devotional

Desiree Fleming

EJF Publishing /Glen Ellyn, Illinois

Copyright © 2016 by **Desiree Fleming**

All rights reserved. No part of this publication may be reproduced, distributed or transmitted in any form or by any means, without prior written permission.

Desiree Fleming/EJF Publishing
Glen Ellyn, Illinois
www.whoops.com

Unless otherwise identified, all Scripture quotations in this publication are taken from the New King James Version (NKJV), New International Version (NIV), Amplified Bible (AMP).

Interior Book Layout © 2016 EJF Publishing
Book Cover Design @2016 www.flamingswordproductions.org
Dance Girl 21-Day Devotion/Desire Fleming. -- 1st ed.
ISBN 9780984179763

Book Dedication

I dedicate this book to my daughter, Elisa.
My favorite little dancer and beautiful flower.
Sweetheart, your dance brings a smile that only you can bring to my face and heart.
Your dance is more than motion, it is the heartbeat of your soul.
I love your creativity for it brings a fresh breath of life.
Throughout life things will change but never allow it to change you.
Keep your dance baby, for it is your freedom and smile!
Share your dance, darling, for it rejuvenates the weak.
Never be afraid to reinvent your dance, for you hold the power to change.

Love,
Mommy

CONTENTS

Peace Is My Dance	9
My New Song Is My Dance	12
Your Purpose Is My Dance	15
Forgiveness Is My Dance	18
Praise Is My Dance	22
Thankfulness Is My Dance	25
Worship Is My Dance	28
Following Your Lord Is My Dance	31
Wisdom and Wealth Is My Dance	35
Self-Control Is My Dance	38
Health Is My Dance	41
Favor Is My Dance	45
Love Is My Dance	48
Balance Is My Dance	52
Knowing Who I Am Is My Dance	56
Restoration Is My Dance	60
Faith Is My Dance	64
Sisterhood Is My Dance	67
Your Will Is My Dance	71
Trusting You Is My Dance	75
Victory Is My Dance	79

Desiree Fleming

Dance Girl 21-Day Devotional

{Day 1}

Peace is My Dance

Good Morning Sister,

In life, we all go through ups and downs, some more than others. Perhaps, last night when you went to bed you had many worries that overwhelmed you. Maybe you had thoughts of decisions and concerns that you just couldn't seem to shake. Do you realize that every day you get up God's mercy is renewed to you? He gives you the gift of peace to overcome yesterday's storms. Today is the beginning of the best days of your life. Today you can choose to be grateful for everything you have and to be thankful even for what you don't have. God is with you.

Scripture: Psalm 118:24

This is the Day the Lord has made; let us rejoice and be glad in it.

The word of God encourages you to rejoice, today and every day. I would like to take this opportunity to implore you to rejoice in the fact that God's peace is your portion. Jesus says he has left peace for you. The peace he has made available to you is irrefutable. I speak the peace of God to your mind, so that you will have a sound mind. Peace is a way of living. Invite peace into your own home and life.

The fact that your Father has blessed you to wake up indicates He has a plan for your day. Our gracious and kind Father is thinking of you. Rejoice before the Lord today by dancing in the face of your yesterday and embracing your today.

Prayer:

Father God, in the Name of Jesus, I thank you for this day that you have made. I ask that you forgive me for when I have not trusted you to be my peace and strength in the midst of the trials I've faced. I trust you Lord and know that Your plan for my life is great. I know that You will give me an expected end, according to Jeremiah 29:11. I dance and bathe in your peace for my life. I receive peace as my dance. In Jesus' Name, Amen.

Dance Girl 21-Day Devotional

Journal Entry

Today's Date_____

Today's Goal...

_____

_____

Who can I share my dance with today...

_____

_____

My personal challenge...

_____

_____

{Day 2}

My New Song Is My Dance

Good Morning Sister,

The word of God encourages you to sing a new song unto the Lord. Do you have a song in your heart? A song of joy, a song of deliverance, a song a praise? Sing, my sister! Do you realize how many people are bound to life's struggles and pressures? When you sing your new song, sing songs of worship and praise, songs that glorify His name. Songs that sing to the essence of who God is in your life, His glorious acts and benefits. Your new song sings about the victory and peace you have.

May the joy of The Lord God be your portion today and every day. Today is a new day, therefore in spite of your current situation joy truly belongs to you. Joy gives you a new song. You no longer have to sings songs of sadness, defeat or misery. This is your time to sing a new song. Sing your new song, sister. Free yourself to sing, dance and rejoice in the new season you are entering.

Scripture: Psalm 96:1-2

1 Sing to the Lord a new song; sing to the Lord, all the earth.
2 Sing to the Lord, praise his name; proclaim his salvation day after day.

Prayer:

Father God, in the name of Jesus, I thank you for my new song. You have given me the room to sing in your presence. Whether I feel I'm on top of the world or in the bottom of the earth, your love for me is very great. And for that I will sing a new song before you, for my new song is my dance. In Jesus' Name. Amen.

Desiree Fleming

Journal Entry

Today's Date_____

Today's Goal...

_____

_____

Who can I share my dance with today...

_____

_____

My personal challenge...

_____

_____

{Day 3}

Your Purpose Is My Dance

Good Morning Sister,

Procrastination is not the way for a vision-minded person. Putting off for tomorrow what can be done today only pushes your plans further and further to the back. You have such an awesome gift to offer the kingdom and the marketplace. God has invested greatness in you; and you have to give birth to it and to continue on with the vision He's given you. Chances are that book, business, meeting, ministry or anything you put off doing today to do tomorrow may continue to get pushed back and placed on the shelf. It will likely sit there and just collect dust. What are you waiting for?

Scripture: Ecclesiastes 11:4

If you wait for perfect conditions, you will never get anything done. God's word informs us not to waste time, waiting for the right time. The right time is now! You don't have time to wait for all the finances to be available, the right moment, the right feeling, the right person to confirm it is God! It's time to let obedience be your dance to get things done, NOW!

Prayer:

Father God, in the name of Jesus, forgive me Father for wasting time waiting on what I believed would be the best time to launch the ministry, write the book, start the business or to feed and clothe the homeless. I will be obedient to the call on my life, knowing that all things are working together for my good. Because I am called according to Your will and purpose, obedience is my dance. In Jesus' Name! Amen.

Dance Girl 21-Day Devotional

Journal Entry

Today's Date_____

Today's Goal...

_____

_____

Who can I share my dance with today...

_____

_____

My personal challenge...

_____

_____

Desiree Fleming

{Day 4}

Forgiveness Is My Dance

Good Morning Sister,

Unforgiveness is an enemy to you as a believer in Christ. It blocks blessings, prayers and the ability to hear from God! Living unforgiveness brings resentment and bitterness. Sometimes, we believe we have forgiven others because we say "I forgive you". But, when the person you "forgave" comes around you can't hardly speak to them or if something they do reminds you of the pain they caused you, you find yourself angry or upset all over again. This may be because there is still unforgiveness.

Unforgiveness puts a hold on your life, your progress, your happiness and your joy. Unforgiveness can actually bring on sickness and depression. Unforgiveness robs you of the opportunity to live your life according to God's plan. It is not God's will for you to be stuck in a place of unforgiveness. I encourage you to give that unforgiveness over to the Father, who sent his son Jesus our priest to die for you so you can be forgiven and forgive others. We must forgive others because Jesus has forgiven us.

Scripture: Matthew 6:14

"If you forgive those who sin against you, your heavenly Father will forgive you."

God gives us the choice of forgiving those who have trespassed against us but we must do this if we want Him to be forgive our sins and trespasses. Yes, someone might have hurt you badly and caused you great stress. Perhaps he cheated on you, or she betrayed your trust, but you are still here. I'm not making light of anything that has happened to you. But your heavenly Father makes it so clear that we have to forgive (release others) so that we too can be released from the sins we have committed and the pain and sorrow that we have caused.

Challenge:

Release the ones who are causing you or have caused you to be in this place. Let them GO!

Prayer:

Father God in the name of Jesus, I come before you with unforgiveness in my heart. It has been so hard for me to let go. I feel that letting _____ (say the person's name) go free makes him/her seem as though what he or she did to me was right. But, God I realize forgiving and releasing _____ actually frees me from the yoke and bondage that unforgiveness brings. Father, I forgive _____. I release _____ and I repent for holding on to this and not trusting You with it. I thank You for forgiving me. Although this pain truly hurts, I choose forgiveness as my dance. In Jesus' Name! Amen!

Dance Girl 21-Day Devotional

Journal Entry

Today's Date_____

Today's Goal...

_____

_____

Who Can I share my dance with today...

_____

_____

My personal challenge...

_____

_____

{Day 5}

Praise Is My Dance

Good Morning Sister,

Praise is one of every Christian's weapons against the enemy. When you praise God it glorifies Him as King of Kings, Lord of Lords, and The Prince of Peace. Praise should always be in our mouths, it should be our common language to adore the most Sovereign Lord! Every praise is due our God, for the marvelous things He has already done in our lives.

Pressures, challenges, and circumstances seem to rob us of giving God praise. May I suggest that you allow these obstacles to push you to send up praise even more. Give God radical praise! Open your mouth and

praise Him. Start today to give thanks and praise unto God. It will set your day off just right. Thanks and praise to God also puts the enemy where he should be, which is right under your feet.

Scripture: Psalm 86:10-13

For thou *art* great and doest wondrous things: thou *art* God alone. Teach me thy way, O LORD; I will walk in thy truth: unite my heart to fear thy name. I will praise thee, O Lord my God, with all my heart: and I will glorify thy name for evermore. For great *is* thy mercy toward me: and thou hast delivered my soul from the lowest hell.

Challenge:

Take time right now and throughout the day to send praise to God.

Prayer:

Father God, in the Name of Jesus, I thank You. I praise you that your love towards me is very great. You have saved me from the depths of death. I am indebted to always praise You! Praise is my song, praise is my way of living, praise is a weapon against the enemy, praise is my dance. I love you, Lord! I praise you, oh Most High King, I honor and adore you, Lord. Be thou glorified and lifted up through my life. In Jesus' Name. Amen.

Desiree Fleming

Journal Entry

Today's Date_____

Today's Goal...

_____

_____

Who can I share my dance with today...

_____

_____

My personal challenge...

_____

_____

{Day 6}

Thankfulness Is My Dance

Good Morning Sister,

You ask what's going on, why haven't things changed! You may be wondering if God is even hearing your prayers, seeing your tears. Trust me He does. It's not over. The fact that you are alive is indicative of His love towards you. He has a plan for you today. In your weakness, His strength is evident.
Are you waiting for God to turn things around for you? I encourage you to take God at His word, knowing that He is the Father of turnarounds. Instead of waiting doing nothing; choose to begin thanking Him for healing you, saving you, delivering you, giving you peace, gracing you to see another day or birthday. Ask Him to remind you of all the ways He's already made. Sometimes, when we are in the midst of a situation we can't remember what God has done. Expect your turnaround! Expect the latter to be greater than what was! Thank Him for Your turnaround!

Scripture: Psalm 95:1-5

Come, let us sing for joy to the Lord; let us shout aloud to the Rock of our salvation.
Let us come before him with thanksgiving and extol him with music and song.
For the Lord is the great God, the great King above all gods.
In his hand are the depths of the earth, and the mountain peaks belong to him.
The sea is his, for he made it, and his hands formed the dry land.

Prayer:

Father God, In the Name of Jesus, I thank you for who You are and all You've already done. You are so amazing! I thank You for Your faithfulness to me, Thank you; today is going to be a great day. You are turning things around on my behalf, being thankful is my dance. In Jesus' Name! Amen!

Dance Girl 21-Day Devotional

Journal Entry

Today's Date_____

Today's Goal...

_____

_____

Who Can I share my dance with today...

_____

_____

My personal challenge...

_____

_____

Desiree Fleming

{Day 7}

Worship Is My Dance

Good Morning Sister,

Contrary to popular belief, worship isn't an experience, a feeling, or a song. Worship is our lifestyle. Worship is your intimate connection with the Father. Commune with Him, lay at His feet, embrace His presence, His glory, embrace His love, live in His presence read His promises to you in His word. Worship God for how He thinks about you, live and breathe His word. Worship Him as you love your husband, children and give to your community.

Worshipping God is an act of our love and affection towards our Father who created and designed us in His own image. Because God is, we worship Him! He is looking for true worshippers!

Scripture: Psalm 95:6-7

Come, let us bow down in worship, let us kneel before the Lord our Maker; for he is our God and we are the people of his pasture, the flock under his care.
John 4:24

God is spirit, and his worshipers must worship in the Spirit and in truth."

Challenge:

Kneel before the Lord, raise your hands, lift your voice unto the Lord. Tell Him just how much He means to you.

Prayer:

Father God, in the awesome and amazing name of Jesus I lift my heart, hands and life to You. I love you, Lord; for your love for me is very great. You created me in Your own image. You called me out of darkness into Your marvelous light. I worship You Father; worship is my dance. Be glorified in Jesus' Name! Amen!

Desiree Fleming

Journal Entry

Today's Date _____

Today's Goal...

_____

_____

Who Can I share my dance with today...

_____

_____

My personal challenge...

_____

_____

{Day 8}

Following You Lord Is My Dance

Good Morning Sister,

What are you hopeful about today? Anything? Today, I encourage you to be hopeful in this: The Lord has a plan just for you, and you are the only one with your assignment. Even though others may be doing things, which are similar to you, they are not the same as what God has given to you to do. You may feel unclear about the path you should take to accomplish what it is that God has called you to do, but don't. Take time this morning to write down what you sense The Lord is saying to you. Write the prophecies you've received.

Perhaps you aren't the type of person who writes things out; perhaps you prefer to just think about it. I would like to share with you the power of writing it.

When you write it, you see it; when you see it, it challenges and motivates you to follow the vision or plan you've written. Think about it, what would life be like if we didn't have God's written word to guide us.

Scripture: Habakkuk 2:2

And the LORD answered me, and said, Write the vision, and make *it* plain upon tables, that he may run that readeth it.

Challenge:

On one of your blank pages label the top part "**Gods' VISION**" then write down what you know or are sensing the Lord is saying for you to do. Obey Him. It may be for you to do now or later. Whichever, keep the vision before you so that it will propel you to go forward.

Prayer:

Father God, in the name of Jesus, I beseech Your throne of grace for my life. My life is not mine. It is the temple of the Holy Spirit, and I ask that you guide me and speak to me regarding Your vision for my life. I desire everything you have for me. I don't want to miss out on any blessing, opportunity, or open door. I thank you for giving me a vision for my life and that I am no stranger to your voice. A stranger's voice I will not follow. I will only follow your voice. I thank you for giving me a plan for my life, knowing your plan for my life is my dance. In Jesus' Name. Amen.

Desiree Fleming

Journal Entry

Today's Date_____

Today's Goal...

_____

_____

Who can I share my dance with today...

_____

_____

My personal challenge...

_____

_____

{Day 9}

Wisdom and Wealth Is My Dance

Good Morning Sister,

Every good and perfect gift comes from above. You are God's' gift to the earth. Every gift He has invested in you is for the kingdom and the market place. The gift you have is to be used to encourage, uplift, heal, and assist others in their path. Others need to see you utilizing the gifts and talents He has invested in you. You are God's great investment, and you have the power to gain wealth.

You may me complaining about what you don't have and what you need. Have you ever evaluated the gifts and talents God has invested in you?

Your gift may be choreographing dances, writing stage plays, administration, coaching, helping, organizing, planning or motivating. Whatever it is, use your talent and expertise to provide food for your table and clothes for your and your family's backs. God wants us to remember Him and that it is He who causes us to gain wealth. It's not your gift. Give it back to Him so he can bless and use it for His glory.

Scripture: Deuteronomy 8:18

But remember the LORD your God, because he is the one who gives you the ability to produce wealth.

Prayer:

Father God, in the matchless name of Jesus. I am so thankful for the gifts and talents you have placed in me and revealed to me through your word and through other confirmation. I thank You that greatness is within me and that You have blessed the work of my hand. Wealth and riches are in my home, I will use it for Your glory. Thank you for causing financial increase to come into my home. Wisdom and wealth are my dance. In Jesus' name. Amen!

Dance Girl 21-Day Devotional

Journal Entry

Today's Date_____

Today's Goal...

_____

_____

Who can I share my dance with today...

_____

_____

My personal challenge...

_____

_____

{Day 10}

Self-Control Is My Dance

Good Morning Sister,

For years I struggled with consuming unhealthy food, sugary beverages, and snacks. Not to mention I had a poor workout regimen. The way I ate suggested to me that I had a lack of self-control, and this was so true. I was out of control in subtle ways. I was a closet eater, going into the cabinet and refrigerator at night eating more than people imagined. If there was cake, I was really bad. I would have my own little cake eating dancing party all alone.

I didn't know how to allow God to guide my eating. I thought I could do it all by myself. But, almost 300 pounds later I found that I needed The Lord to help me. You are not alone in your struggle, whether it's overspending, overeating, compulsive talking or impulsive behavior, God's grace is sufficient for the struggle. The Lord guides us and he satisfies our mouths, and through Him our youth is renewed like eagle's. We can soar through these struggles when we yield to Jesus. Don't give in to the battle, ask the Father to help you walk in discipline/self-control in the areas you are struggling.

Scripture: Psalm 103:5

Who satisfieth thy mouth with good *things; so that* thy youth is renewed like the eagle's.

Prayer:

Father God, I come before You in Jesus' name. Lord, I wrestled and struggled with this addiction for a long time. I have not been able to shake it off by myself. But father, I know, according to Your word, Jesus bore all of my sicknesses, afflictions, and griefs on the cross. Father, I yield my body to you. It belongs to You. Guide me continually, Lord; satisfy my mouth. I profess with my mouth I live a disciplined lifestyle. Self-control is my dance. In Jesus' name I pray. Amen!

Desiree Fleming

Journal Entry

Today's Date_____

Today's Goal...

_____

_____

Who can I share my dance with today...

_____

_____

My personal challenge...

_____

_____

{Day 11}

Health Is My Dance

Good Morning Sister,

Without "you", there is no you! (Selah) Is everybody else needing you to put out the little fires in their lives? Have you become the go to woman for everything? On the outside you seem to have it together, however inwardly you are breaking down little by little, day by day and minute by minute? God sees you and never intended for you to carry the weight of others on your back, we are to bear the infirmities of others but not be the one who solves their problems, change their circumstances. Burnout is not for you, my sister. You cannot forget about "you" in the process of helping to serve others. I truly believe we are called by God to serve, but not to the place of no return where we forget our household and health.

Don't die before your time. God will give you strength and grace for the journey. You can't go without spiritually, mentally, physically and emotionally taking care of yourself.

Challenge:

Spiritually: Take time daily to spend with The Father before you get out of the bed. Ask Him to guide your day and show you what you should and shouldn't do, so that He will be glorified. (He gets no pleasure in you being burned out)

Mentally: Take time to relax. Spend time resting in God's presence. Spend time with friends that are good for you and who pour good seeds of encouragement and laughter into your life.

Physically: Take some time a few days of the week for physical activity that you enjoy doing. Perhaps it's dancing, walking, stepping. Whatever it is get your physical body together.

Emotionally: Get up in the morning and clean yourself up, wash your face, put on a fragrance that makes you smile, find something bright to wear. Protect yourself from conversations that drain you.

Scripture: 3rd John 1:2

Beloved, I wish above all things that thou mayest prosper and be in health, even as thy soul prospereth.

God not only wants you to prosper financially, He wants your soul to prosper. When you take care of yourself, spiritually, mentally, emotionally and physically you cause your soul to prosper.

Prayer:

Father God in the name of Jesus, I thank You for speaking directly to my soul today. I'm thankful that you desire to see me happy and not crazy and without hope. Father, You are my hope. I choose to live. I choose to love myself. I choose the life of joy You have predestined for me to live. Health is my dance; I rejoice in the fact that I have a choice to live. In Jesus' Name! Amen!

Desiree Fleming

Journal Entry

Today's Date_____

Today's Goal...

_____

_____

Who Can I share my dance with today...

_____

_____

My personal challenge...

_____

_____

{Day 12}

Favor Is My Dance

Good Morning Sister,

What do you think is holding you back from finishing school, going to school, getting a better job/different career or starting over? It's fear! God says perfect love casts out all fear. That's His love perfected in us. Learning to trust God cancels fear and the anxieties that come along with it.

Fear can be a silent but dominating force. A force which can hinder you from progressing or being successful in life. Fear of the unknown, fear of success, fear of what if it doesn't work out or if it doesn't work out the way you hoped for it to work out. The enemy sees your potential and entertains you with thoughts of "I can't do that!", "It won't work for me!", "Somebody else can do it better than me!", "He's not really into me!" Listen, if you are entertaining these thoughts you have to start canceling them, because they are an enemy of your future, your today, and God's' word.

Fear is the opposite of faith. I encourage you today to change the way you think. Instead of saying it can't be done, say "I can do all things through Christ who gives me strength.

Scripture: Joshua 1:9

Have I not commanded you? Be strong and courageous. Do not be afraid; do not be discouraged, for the Lord your God will be with you wherever you go. Everything God has called you to do will have a little anxiety around it, but it's not God's plan for you to wear that fear or live in it. His word instructs you to do what He says and He's going to be with you Wherever you go! That's something to dance about right now. You are not going on your own. Your Daddy/Father is going right with you.

Prayer:

Father God in the name of Jesus, I truly thank You that I no longer have to live in fear. You have anointed me with favor to pursue what You've called me to do. I confess that I am Yours and you are mine, I walk by faith and not by what I feel or even see. You are the God of my yesterday, my today, and my future. I rejoice that fear is under my feet. I resist the enemy of my future and rest in You! Favor is my dance. It is so, In Jesus' Name! Amen!

Dance Girl 21-Day Devotional

Journal Entry

Today's Date_____

Today's Goal...

_____

_____

Who can I share my dance with today...

_____

_____

My personal challenge...

_____

_____

{Day 13}

Love Is My Dance

Good Morning Sister,

Being Christ-like after someone has let you down and betrayed you, that is one hard feat. Betrayal is something no woman desires, hopes for or would ever want to experience. When a woman feels betrayed the spiraling effect can be so devastating that it can cause her to almost be at the point of no return, depending on the severity of the betrayal. Could you imagine that someone you love so dearly and have shared your secrets and most intimate moments with sharing what you've only confided in them with others?

To be Christ-like is to love those who have hurt you and done you wrong. We even have to love those who feel justified in their wrongdoing. It might've been your spouse, sibling, friend, parent, co-worker, child or family member; and you just can't understand why. Truthfully, sometimes there is no concrete answer.

However, there is a solution. I'm not suggesting that you do this, but Jesus had fellowshipped, broke bread with, preached the gospel to and with his betrayer. Jesus gave us the perfect example of not allowing others actions, even when against us to turn evil for evil. If you allow what they did to you to keep you from being able to love them or forgive them, you're giving it too much power to define you.

Scripture: Matthew 26:14-16

14 Then one of the Twelve—the one called Judas Iscariot—went to the chief priests 15 and asked, "What are you willing to give me if I deliver him over to you?" So they counted out for him thirty pieces of silver. 16 From then on Judas watched for an opportunity to hand him over.

Luke 22:47-51
47 While he was still speaking a crowd came up, and the man who was called Judas, one of the Twelve, was leading them. He approached Jesus to kiss him, 48 but Jesus asked him, "Judas, are you betraying the Son of Man with a kiss?" 49 When Jesus' followers saw what was going to happen, they said, "Lord, should we strike with our swords?" 50 And one of them struck the servant of the high priest, cutting off his right ear. 51 But Jesus answered, "No more of this!" And he touched the man's ear and healed him.

Challenge:

After reading how Jesus healed the high priest's servant's ear what do you think your response should be to someone who betrays you? My hope is that it would be like Jesus' response. You still have to be who God created you to be. If the person who betrayed you needs prayer, food, clothes, or a kind word, you should be able to offer it to them.

Prayer:

Father God, I thank You for teaching me how to be Christ-like, even when I don't understand or agree with what others have done to me. Jesus showed me that life isn't about getting even, but getting to the other side and rising up from what looks like the bottom. Jesus healed one of his wood-be captors even when he was on his way to death. I thank you for grace to touch others as Christ did. Love is my dance. In Jesus' Name! Amen.

Dance Girl 21-Day Devotional

Journal Entry

Today's Date_____

Today's Goal...

_____

_____

Who can I share my dance with today...

_____

_____

My personal challenge...

_____

_____

Desiree Fleming

{Day 14}

Balance Is My Dance

Good Morning Sister,

Hectic schedule today? What do you have going this morning? Cooking, washing, getting the kids ready, packing lunches, making sure you have your husband's clothes taken care of? Have a deadline to meet? Whew, that's a lot. And that might not be all if you consider what you didn't get to last night.

With all you have going on, did you forget to take time with your Daddy? He will help you to create the balance you need as a mother, wife, businesswoman, church or community member. Here is a suggestion, stop whatever you're doing right now and breathe. Invite God into the business of your life. Ask Him for guidance. We know mothers and wives have to juggle hectic schedules, especially if they have active families.

The only way to strike balance is to create it. God helps us to create that balance. He says seek Him first and everything else you need will be added to you. This is a daily "seek" to have everything needed, daily. Therefore, if you need more time in the day, He will help you come up with a realistic schedule, one which includes Him first thing in the morning and rest for you.

Scripture: Proverbs 16:9

A man's heart plans his way, But the Lord directs his steps.

Challenge:

Think about what you have to accomplish today. Now think about if you should be trying to do it all by yourself. Once you see that you are doing too much on your own, you must be willing to let go of some of the extra activities you're involved in. Maybe even some of the stuff you do for your kids.
Remember, it's not God's will for you to try to do it all on your own. Give yourself permission to take a break EVERYDAY, even if it's just 5 minutes in the bathroom, or a 10-minute walk without your phone.

Prayer:

Daddy, I thank You that you are here with me. I thank you that balance is my dance. I am not crumbling under the pressure anymore. I am going to intentionally get up a little earlier to spend time with You for my life and the life of my family. Lord, I need You to help me strike balance. Show me how to start today. I will listen for your voice throughout this day and every day. I thank you for teaching me how to live in balance. I choose balance as my dance. In Jesus' Name! Amen.

Dance Girl 21-Day Devotional

Journal Entry

Today's Date _____

Today's Goal...

_____

_____

Who can I share my dance with today...

_____

_____

My personal challenge...

_____

_____

Desiree Fleming

{Day 15}

Knowing Who I Am Is My Dance

Good Morning Sister,

Who are you? Who do they say you are? How do people view you? Does it really matter what they say? Finding your identity can be a life-challenging crisis, lasting a long time. You may think you are just his wife, their mother, their child, a teacher, a nurse, bartender, friend, preacher, or whatever. The real question should be, who does God say you are, and how does He see you?

If you've always been told you're nothing, you will never be anything, you've gone as far as you can go, you're getting too old and have embraced others confessions for you, it's challenging to know what God is saying concerning you. Especially, if you've always valued others opinions.

Knowing who you are is so essential to the work God has placed in your hands. Today, choose to focus more on who and what God says and less on what others say. It will begin to transform your life. You may wonder what God is saying about you. The best way to find out what God says is to read His word and begin to confess what His word says. For example: His word says "I am more than a conqueror", "I am a lender not a borrower", "I am the head and not the tail", "I am beautifully and wonderfully made", "I am healed and whole", "I am an overcomer", "I shall live and not die", "I declare the wondrous works of the Lord". You see, once you begin to speak God's word concerning you, it gives you identity. You will begin to walk in Godly boldness and not be timid. You will declare and live out what God says you are. When you dance in the awesomeness of who God says you are that's when you'll find fulfillment and contentment in your life.

Scripture: Psalm 139:14

I praise you because I am fearfully and wonderfully made; your works are wonderful; I know that full well.

Challenge:

You might not see yourself the way God created and predestined you to be. But as you began to speak His word, you will call into existence who you are meant to be. Not who or what you were, but WHO HE says you are. Find three scriptures that speak the total opposite of the negative things you believe about yourself. Keep speaking them throughout today and every day, expect manifestation.

Prayer:

Father God, in the name of Jesus, I thank You for giving me an identity in you. Knowing who I am in you, is my dance. I am not just a wife, mother, employee, businesswoman, or friend. I am chosen and predestined to do great exploits in the earth for Your glory. Use me Lord, change me, make me over and have Your way in me, in the Name of Jesus, it is so! AMEN!

Dance Girl 21-Day Devotional

Journal Entry

Today's Date_____

Today's Goal...

_____

_____

Who can I share my dance with today...

_____

_____

My personal challenge...

_____

_____

{Day 16}

Restoration Is My Dance

Good Morning Sister,

GET UP! YES, YOU! GET UP! Are you seriously going to just sit there like you have no purpose, or like God hasn't brought you through before? Maybe nobody ever told you this but, every woman experiences crisis in life. That crisis does not determine your outcome. The enemy would have you to believe that it does, but it does not.

The devil comes to kill, steal, and destroy you, your purpose, your dream and your destiny. He wants you to give up on every glimpse that looks like hope, because it is the very thing that could possibly take you over into your promised land. He would love for you to just give up and die. He probably even told you to just die. But, the spirit of Life inside of you will not let you go down that path.

Yeah, you look like you are defeated. Yeah, you feel depressed, but God sees you differently. He sees you as a victor not a victim, successful not impoverished, healthy and whole, not sick. You have to tell yourself to obey God's word and "GET UP." The floor should only be for kneeling to pray, not for staying down, "GET UP!"

Scripture: Romans 8:37

37 Nay, in all these things we are more than conquerors through him that loved us.
You are more than that sickness, you are more than that divorce, you are more than that failed business, you are more than that missed opportunity, you are more than that loss. You are more than a conqueror. Conquerors fight until the end. Get up in your prayer closet, speak the word and command the enemy off your stuff. Jesus has already won the battle; it's time for you to abide in Him and Get Up. He rose so you could know it's possible to get up out of what looks like a dead situation. Get UP! Just like He did!

Prayer:

Father, I believe. Help thou my unbelief. I speak what your word says and I believe that I am more than a conqueror. I am an overcomer, I am blessed and highly favored, I am your daughter and you are my daddy, who always causes me to triumph over the enemy. I thank You that I can hide in the shadow of Your wings, and You protect me from every fiery dart that has tried to defeat me. Restoration is my dance. I render satan powerless over me and cancel his assignment to suppress, depress, and oppress me in Jesus' Name! AMEN!

Dance Girl 21-Day Devotional

Journal Entry

Today's Date_____

Today's Goal...

_____

_____

Who can I share my dance with today...

_____

_____

My personal challenge...

_____

_____

{Day 17}

Faith Is My Dance

Good Morning Sister,

What are you believing God for right now? Maybe it's been years and you have believed God was going to do it, but you are beginning to lose hope. You know what, if God has spoken it in His Word He will bring it to pass. His word is what he's given us to place our faith in. Without His word we can't know what He's able to do.

The enemy wants you to stop believing, to just let go. But, I encourage you today to believe again, dream again, envision again. Activate your faith begin speaking God's word that confirms what He has spoken to you. Speak His word into the atmosphere; it's already established in heaven so release it in the earth realm. God responds to His word when released in faith. Believe Him again!

Scripture: 1st John 5:14

This is the confidence we have in approaching God: that if we ask anything according to his will, he hears us.

Hebrews 11:1

Now Faith is the confidence in what we hope for and the assurance about what we do not see.

Prayer:

Father God, I believe Your word. I choose to see differently. I choose to be an exception to the norm. I believe what Your word says. I repent and renounce all doubt and empty words that I've released in the earth realm. I bring every thought into captivity and denounce faithless acts in Jesus' Name! Father, I believe by faith that what you have for me, it is for me. I believe that Your divine will for my life shall be done. NOW Faith is my dance. I call forth every blessing you have released to me and receive it, in Jesus' Name! Amen!

Journal Entry

Today's Date_____

Today's Goal...

_____

_____

Who can I share my dance with today...

_____

_____

My personal challenge...

_____

_____

{Day 18}

Sisterhood Is My Dance

Good Morning Sister,

Sisterhood is one of the ultimate dances of a woman's success. But friendships for women can be such a challenge. We have so many issues to work through. Celebrating other women: our peers, older and younger, should be something we strive to do on a regular basis. When you can't compliment, encourage, motivate and inspire other women you have to do a self-check.

What about her makes you feel insecure? What is it that she does that you wish you could do? What about her makes you feel inadequate? What has she done to you that stops you from celebrating her success?

Even if you have an answer to each one of the questions listed above, they still do not warrant you not celebrating your sister. We in the body of Christ must move past our flesh and begin to push others. It's so vital to embrace the gifts that God has placed around us in our sisters and in one another. Even if you feel that you embrace others but you don't get it in return.

I encourage you to pray and to ask God to connect you with other sisters who will pour into you and push you. Sisters who will celebrate the gem you are and the anointing and gifts you bring to the friendship, women who you may be able to work with to enhance the kingdom of God.

Scripture: 1 Corinthians 3:9
For we are co-workers together in God's service; you are God's field, God's building.

Ephesians 4:16

He makes the whole body fit together perfectly. As each part does its own special work, it helps the other parts grow, so that the whole body is healthy and growing and full of love.

Challenge:

Think about a person you admire, but may be intimidated by her success and confidence. Compliment her and share how you appreciate her gift to the body of Christ and/ or the community.

Prayer:

Father God, in the Name of Jesus help me to walk in humility and love toward my sisters in the body of Christ. Remove everything from me that causes me to not celebrate my sisters. I repent for harboring selfishness, hatred, bitterness, disappointment and any resentment. I choose to love and celebrate who my sisters are in You, because they are my sisters and Your daughters. We are joint heirs with Christ and we make up different parts of Your body. Thank you for my sisters. Healed and wholesome relationships are my dance. Thank you for calling me to love greater. In Jesus' Name! Amen!

Desiree Fleming

Journal Entry

Today's Date_____

Today's Goal...

_____

_____

Who can I share my dance with today...

_____

_____

My personal challenge...

_____

_____

{Day 19}

Your Will Is My Dance

Good Morning Sister,

Frustration sometimes seems as if it is a way of life. When in all actuality it isn't. However, there is a frustration (an agitation) which exists to get you to see that this isn't the way life is supposed to be lived. It should cause you to decide this isn't the way God predestined me to live.

If you're experiencing any kind of unexplainable frustration, you can believe the Holy Spirit is probably at work trying to get you to make the needed changes to fulfill your kingdom assignment; the thing or things God has ordained for you to do. This frustration/agitation may be pushing the button of overeating, attitude adjustment, selfishness, lack, or being to overly committed to what's not connected to your destiny. Whatever it is, recognize it for what it really is, a call to move you to make a needed change toward your purpose. God is looking for you to come to Him with this agitation, so that he can help direct you.

Scripture: Romans 12:1

Therefore, I urge you, brothers and sisters, in view of God's mercy, to offer your bodies as a living sacrifice, holy and pleasing to God--this is your true and proper worship.

Challenge:

Take time to prayerfully submit your body and thoughts to the Lord this morning and throughout this month.

Perhaps, you've been considering changing the way you respond to others, because the way you respond continuously creates conflict. It seems to cause distance between you and your family, friends or coworkers. The frustration is there to push you to change.

Prayer:

Father God in the name of Jesus, I submit my ways to you. Have your way in me, Lord. Change me from the inside out. I submit to the change you have awaiting me. Even when I feel I'm in the right but might be wrong, I submit to you. My mind, my mouth, my heart, my life belongs to you. I commit and submit myself to you. I thank you that your voice and your will is my dance. In Jesus' Name! Amen.

Desiree Fleming

Journal Entry

Today's Date_____

Today's Goal...

_____

_____

Who can I share my dance with today...

_____

_____

My personal challenge...

_____

_____

{Day 20}

Trusting You Is My Dance

Good Morning Sister,

Being smack dab in the middle–Transitions–can be one of the most complicated places to be. Transitions don't always ask for permission to come, they just show up unexpected. Sometimes we plan transitions. But those we don't plan can be challenging and conflicting.

You may be in the transition of moving or going into a new career. You may be experiencing relationship changes. You may be having changing thoughts, plans, or ideas. Whatever or whichever it is, TRUST God! When you don't know what to do, you give God an awesome opportunity to show Himself strong and mighty. You can see Him as Father and who His word says He is.

Could you imagine the transition of losing your husband, being in debt over your head, not a dime to pay the lights, gas, rent, car note and the debtors say we are turning it all off and coming to get your only means of getting to a job or finding one? When the woman in 2nd King 4 husband died and there was debt to be paid, the price was put on her two sons head. But, she didn't just give in to the fear and anxiety this change was taking her through she went to the man of God Elisha and he gave her directions of how to pay her debt and keep her sons from being sold into slavery. She had to believe/trust God that this transition didn't come to destroy her. I'm sure she cried, I'm sure she was afraid, but she didn't have time to go into a pity party while changes had taken place in her family status. God took what little she had a "but a jar of oil" multiplied it, paid her debts, all during her transition and left her with a surplus. (Please take time to study this passage)

You as God's daughter have to trust that in spite of the complexities of your life that God will make a way.

Scripture: Proverbs 3:5
Trust in the LORD with all your heart and lean not on your own understanding.

Challenge:

Work on not trying to figure it out; work on leaning on God's word, that's how we learn to trust Him. In spite of the transition you're currently experiencing, trust God with all your heart, realizing He will not fail you.

Prayer:

Father God, in the name of Jesus, I truly don't understand why and what's going on in my life, but what I realize is that in spite of the changes I'm experiencing, I choose to trust You. Lord. I know you know what's best for me. I come in alignment with trusting you, knowing you have my back. I will not lean to my own understanding, knowing that You have already worked everything out. Lord, I thank you that I have a new dance and that dance is to trust you! In Jesus Name! Amen!

Desiree Fleming

Journal Entry

Today's Date_____

Today's Goal...

_____

_____

Who can I share my dance with today...

_____

_____

My personal challenge...

_____

_____

{Day 21}

Victory Is My Dance

Good Morning Sister,

Dance, **D**ance, **D**ance! You have every right to dance today and every day. With every trial you've come through: failed relationship, challenging childhood, divorce, sexual abuse, mental, physical, emotional and/or economical abuse. You have come through too much not to dance all over the enemy's head. In spite of what it looked like, you made it! When you told yourself and others told you it was over, you made it! You are one of God's greatest gifts to the body of Christ.

Dance because your best days are now and ahead of you! Dance because you are healed! Dance because you are free! Dance because you are victorious! Dance because God is Good! Dance because you owe God your dance! Dance because He wouldn't let you die when you had given up! Dance because greater is He that's in you than He that's in the world! Dance my sister, DANCE!

Praise is your dance! Your song is your dance! Worship is your dance! Forgiveness is your dance! Healing is your dance! Deliverance is your dance! Success is your Dance! Victory is your dance! Joy is your dance! Happiness is your dance!

Scriptures: Exodus 15:20

Miriam the prophetess, Aaron's sister, took the timbrel in her hand, and all the women went out after her with timbrels and with dancing.

Psalm 30:11
You have turned for me my mourning into dancing; You have loosed my sackcloth and girded me with gladness.

Psalm 149:3
Let them praise His name with dancing; Let them sing praises to Him with timbrel and lyre. **Dance Girl!**

Dance Girl 21-Day Devotional

Journal Entry

Today's Date _____

Today's Goal...

_____

_____

Who can I share my dance with today...

_____

_____

My personal challenge...

_____

_____

ABOUT THE AUTHOR

Desiree Fleming, affectionately known as Lady Des, has been married over 25 years, mother of two beautiful children, grandmother, and blessed to raise her late sisters' children. She is a family woman, evangelist, empowerment coach, author, playwright, and executive director of "Women Helping Others Overcome Personal Struggles" and "YEP! It's A Wrap! Productions."

Other Publications

"Unapologetically Woman "A Woman Without Regrets Or Excuses" (Book Collaboration)
"Where Could I Take My Shame "The Unprotected Daughter"

Willow Series:
"Meet Willow" children's book
"Everybody Gets It Except Willow" OR So She Thinks" (Co-written with her daughter Elisa)

www.ingramcontent.com/pod-product-compliance
Lightning Source LLC
Chambersburg PA
CBHW050605300426
44112CB00013B/2083